When the Breakup
Has No Makeup,
It Is Time to Wake Up!

When the Breakup Has No Makeup, It Is Time to Wake Up!

P.H. Jones

Cover design by
Buddha Cowboy Productions
Ty Donaldson
www.buddhacowboy.com

Thank you for the loving support and creativity of Xlibris Team.

Library of Congress Control Number:		2010916547
ISBN:	Hardcover	978-1-4568-1069-6
	Softcover	978-1-4568-1068-9
	Ebook	978-1-4568-1070-2

This book was printed in the United States of America.

To order additional copies of this book, contact:
Xlibris Corporation
1-888-795-4274
www.Xlibris.com
Orders@Xlibris.com
86880

Contents

DEDICATION

I dedicate this book to my family and friends for all their support during my time of struggle that changed my life forever. To my husband, Frank, you have taught me to love and trust again and to have moral courage; I will love you forever. To my son, Jacob, you are my strength and my blessing; I love you beyond measure, and I am very proud of you. Last but not least, to my first love, Jesus, I could not have gotten to the other side without you; thank you for hearing my prayers and restoring me, healing my broken heart, removing the brokenness inside, and giving me faith and strength to stand up and live again.

I will always praise your name.
I now have a sense of purpose because of all of you. What was meant to destroy me, God has used it all for my good.

Forever grateful,
XOXO

Introduction

As we all travel through life, we all gather stories to tell of our adventures and life lessons.

Through these experiences, whichever one is more exciting or painful, you decide to document them in a journal. Then one day, without even thinking about it, you decide it's time to share a few of these thoughts with others. So putting pen to paper or fingers to keyboard, you begin to make sense of the experience, and before you know it, you have written your first book. This is just the short version of why and how writing this book came to pass.

The story you are about to read is about my experience, *When the Breakup Has No Makeup, It Is Time to Wake Up*. Through the intense struggle of trying to make the relationship work, it became the nightmare that I thought I would never wake up from. When we go into a marriage or relationship, we don't think about what would happen if we break up. We all get so obsessed with the passion and love we can't ever imagine that our relationship would ever end in a breakup. Well, that is what happens, but after the months of pain, tears, anger, fear, resentment, loneliness, abuse, etc., something happened; something that made me wake up!

My faith had been rocked, hammered, stolen, ripped away, and I had no confidence in myself, and I did not trust anyone, so I began to pray with fervent prayer asking for God to forgive me for not being able to keep my commitment to the vows that I had taken. I had to take it one sunrise at a time. When I would wake each day and the pain was still there, I began to think there is a lesson here that I must learn from, and I don't ever want to repeat it ever again. So I began to keep a journal and relive the pain of all the events. Prayer was my only friend, and through all the sleepless nights of tears, I began to experience forgiveness toward those that had hurt me. But most of all, I began to forgive myself, then this small flame that represents my faith was burning inside of me; it started to ignite into a burning ember, then a new fire of passion—with compassion, wisdom, forgiveness, joy, peace and, most of all, love—embraced me, held me, and helped me stand up again. I had come back to my first love that is the Lord, and he forgave me and made me whole again.

I wish I could say that this happened overnight, but it took several months, but I believe if it would have happened quickly, I may not have learned the lesson. I have learned many life lessons from this one journey. As I look back now, I would not change a thing; well, maybe a few things. I have learned so much about myself; I have gained discipline, respect, gratefulness, boundaries, listening skills, patience, and so many more amazing treasures that I have written about in this book.

My main motivation in sharing this information is to help others in their time of need when they are going through the fire of a breakup that has no makeup. I can promise you that if you apply what you learn in this book and make the effort, you will find yourself taking a stand and feeling like you can live, love, and laugh again. Your faith will be renewed, and you will have your own journal to share with others.

When the Breakup Has No Makeup, It Is Time to Wake Up is a mental boot camp that deals with the emotional pain of being in a relationship that has no fiber to hold it together any longer. The boot camp, like any boot camp, has some tough love, so take your ego and put it in a closet and get ready to be set free. Learning to listen, bend, have boundaries, and to persevere to a new beginning is gratifying and humbling at the same time. Being true to yourself and finding the authentic you. It all does not happen in one day, but with prayer and action, you will see healing in your heart. I am evidence of God's mercy on my life, and I believe that with God all things are possible. Time can change you, but you can't change time or the past. Look into your tomorrows with big goals and visions, and expect a miracle. Find your sense of purpose, and do it.

God bless
P J xo

When the Breakup Has No Makeup, It Is Time to Wake Up

Is it destiny driving this course?

Why is this happening?

What happened to our promise to each other?

Letting go of something that felt so right that makes a turn that becomes so wrong. What happened? You never saw it coming. Then this crushing pressure in your chest makes you feel like you're having a heart attack.

The pain is so deep that words cannot express the loss.

The only cure at this point is to *stop*!

To stop what you are doing and realize it is not a dream, but the moment of reality that someone you loved is leaving your life forever.

With this breakup, there is *no* making up; a new chapter is about to begin in your life, and it is up to you to learn from this season of pain. You must wake up and clean up the broken pieces to create a new beginning!

You may ask yourself "Is that possible?" Well, the answer is yes.

The concept of this book is to help you learn how to live, love, and laugh again. So the best way to exercise this was to create a mental boot camp. At this boot camp, we are going to do a lot of cleaning up; there will be some tough love, *aah* moments, funny memories, but no more pity parties. But there will be changes in the way that you think, talk, and listen. It will be fun if you make the effort. So put on your best smile, turn off the television, grab your reading glasses if you need them, a tissue, and your favorite beverage, and let's get started.

Welcome to Boot Camp Cleanup

At BCCU, we have a checklist of details that need addressing, and changes are about to be made to repair, restore, and reclaim your life. This is known as the RR&R; this will be the new motto of your next season of life. You are about to be given many treasures of wisdom that will follow you for many years to come, if you apply the effort.

BCCU is not a miracle drug, but it has miraculous healing lessons that will take you from the torment of a broken heart to the gratefulness of lessons that have been learned; it will teach you to fly like an eagle. To spread your new wings and soar in all areas of your life.

Remember, BCCU is not easy; cleaning up any mess is a job, and if it was easy, then everyone would be doing it, and there would be no purpose for this book!

How to Use This Book

Take one day at a time, but do at least three of the new RR&R—repair, restore, and reclaim—every day, along with PP&P—perseverance, patience, and prayer.

Please take down notes in your book; use it like a journal. When a paragraph or a word touches your heart, take note, underline the words, and use them like a seed to plant into your heart. Some of the sections may be short, but use the space to put down your own thoughts; you will be glad you did. You will see your growth and healing in your own words.

Throughout this book, you will have new rules, boundaries, quotes, scriptures, and prayers that will guide you through the lessons. With all new lessons, you will have to make a decision that only you can make. If you want something to change in your life, *you* have to change.

Let's get started!

Rule 1:   Quitters never win, winners never quit!

Prayer: Lord God, in Jesus's name, thank you for this amazing day that you have made. Let us rejoice and be glad in it! Thank you for my perfect health, financial provision, blessed life, your Holy Spirit, family and friends and, most of all, you, for loving me and forgiving me and giving me another chance to make a difference. Talk with you later. I love you! Amen.

On our first day of BCCU, let's just be grateful and thankful. We can modify our prayer more to our heart as the mending process begins. Let's keep it simple, and God will lead us on our path as the healing starts to repair the brokenness and pain. It is a process, and there are many parts to repair.

Here are the first thirteen words on the list that start the repair process:

- Forgiveness
- Ask in prayer
- Humble thyself
- Bend
- Heal
- No
- Boundaries
- Gratefulness
- Compassion
- Tears to fill a river
- No vices!
- Don't curse others or yourself!
- Be still, bridle your tongue (this is the hardest one), learn to listen

Only thirteen words of exciting treasures of wisdom and fourteen little rules to help repair the brokenness in your heart. And once you get these down with a little help from PP&P (perseverance, patience, and prayer), the best is yet to come.

But first let me explain each word so you completely understand the importance of each repair that will soon take place. It is a miracle once they have taken hold; the transformation and healing begins to change your life beyond your understanding. This transformation will take you to the next level of your journey.

_____

_____

_____

_____

_____

_____

_____

_____

_____

_____

Rule 2:   If you don't have anything nice to say about anyone, then don't say it at all.

Also if you hear someone speaking poorly about someone, excuse yourself and leave!

Forgiveness: The best answer is because God told us to forgive one another because he has forgiven us!

You may be asking "How? The pain is so deep, look what they did to me! Why? What did I do to deserve this?"

Forgiveness is a gift; as we get deeper into the healing, you will see this gift start to transform in your heart and spirit. It is truly a treasure that you must guard. Without forgiveness, the root of bitterness in your heart can destroy you and cause years of harm to you and to others due to your actions. The anger, hatefulness, selfishness will take over your spirit and create disease in your body. Forgiveness is not hard if you are willing. It is a process, but with God, all things are possible. Press forward for the goal, which is the healing of your heart, and peace and joy will follow along with many blessings upon your life.

Once you open the door to forgiveness, the rest of the actions you take to clean up your life will be like precious pearls—priceless.

_____

_____

_____

_____

_____

_____

_____

_____

_____

Rule 3: Prayer is a privilege.

Ask in prayer: So many hopes and dreams are not answered due to the lack of prayer requests, fear of asking, or not knowing what to ask; we are children of the Most High God, and he wants to hear from us no matter what the situation or request. It is better to have asked than not. When we ask, we must be willing to accept the answer. Sometimes prayers are not answered for our own good, and with time, we will be thankful for those unanswered prayers. But we must always remember that prayers are answered in God's timing, not ours. He knows best. When praying for the healing of your heart, you must know that you will be tested. This is why it is a process due to our own free will. You will hear me say this more than once in this book that you are your own worst enemy when it comes to being obedient and sticking to the program. That is why you are reading BCCU to keep you in line when the going gets tough.

Rule 4:   Always begin and finish your day with a prayer of gratefulness.

Humble thyself: To be humble is an act of dying to self. When you lay down your control and accept what must be done to improve the situation, it will entail some changes to happen inside of you. Know that with change, new opportunities will be on your pathway. Humbling thyself will begin with a quietness in your spirit that will teach you to listen more deeply, choose your words more carefully, and have more respect for others. Learning to live, love, and laugh again will begin once you humble thyself.

_____

_____

_____

_____

_____

_____

_____

_____

_____

_____

Rule 5:   Learn the rules of the game before you play; the outcome will be more rewarding.

Bend: When you stop bending and stretching, for example, your body will become very stiff. Aches and pains in your body will become a daily grind in your life. When the heart is broken, you must not harden your heart with hatred and put up walls. This will only cause more pain and multiple problems. Learning to listen is the beginning of learning to bend. If not, you will break. Warning, when getting advice from others, be sure that the advice is good advice.

You may be wondering how you'll know when it's good advice. So many people will have opinions, but it may not be good advice; this is where learning to listen is very important. The words they are saying should have a positive motivation and deal with a solution, not create a bigger problem.

If the person giving you advice has not lived through this situation before, they may not have the compassion to understand the pain that you are dealing with, so guard your heart. Their intention may be from the heart, but they can cause more harm than good. When you share information, be sure that you can trust the person that you are telling it to. Remember you are in a healing process, and everything you do and say can be used against you.

_____
_____
_____
_____
_____
_____
_____
_____
_____
_____

Rule 6: When you don't feel well, take care of yourself.

Heal: Healing is a process; the physical body can heal and restore itself with time. A broken arm or leg can heal if set properly and given time to heal. If not, the bones will not heal properly and problems will follow you for many years to come. A broken heart can heal, but it does take time and effort to heal properly. There are thirteen steps to healing; each step brings you closer to repairing your broken heart. Following these suggestions can change your life forever.

_____

_____

_____

_____

_____

_____

_____

_____

_____

_____

_____

Rule 7: What two-letter word has the power to save your life?

No: Wow! This is such a small word that has so much power. This word needs to be used more in our vocabulary. We must learn not to be people pleasers, allowing things to happen that are not acceptable. When we bend our knees to bad behavior, it will at some point cross our paths and hurt us. If you look back in your relationship, you will see that things were happening that were unacceptable and you did not speak up to confront the situation. What you have learned now is to say no!

Now that this breakup has no makeup, learn from your past mistakes and move forward. At word number 6, you can feel the pull on your heartstrings, and it's time to take a deep breath, wipe away the tears and fears, and say to yourself, "I forgive myself and those that have hurt me. I want my life back with beauty from ashes."

Rule 8: Have you ever wondered why the ocean in all its mass and power stops right at the shoreline?

Boundaries: This is my favorite; it's one of the top five most important strengths to have in your life, but it's also one of the hardest, if you have never had it. Boundaries are shields for protection. Boundaries are the rules of the game. You must have guidelines to follow to accomplish your goals. We will suggest more ideas of boundaries and how to address them during the healing process later in this book.

_____

_____

_____

_____

_____

_____

_____

_____

_____

_____

Rule 9:   Helping others will make your problems seem small.

Gratefulness: Every new day that we are blessed to have breath in our lungs means that God has given us a new beginning.

Start each morning with a prayer of gratefulness and thanksgiving, which will ignite your spirit with peace. Being grateful is an amazing feeling where at times words cannot express. As your heart begins to heal, this wonderful emotion of gratefulness will give you an openness and understanding that will give you clarity to see the path you are on and where you are going. You may also at this point see that even though the breakup caused so much change and pain in your life, it has given you another chance to grow and learn life lessons that you may not have embraced. Life lessons are priceless jewels. You cannot buy them; you must live them!

Rule 10: Learn the lesson and don't repeat! To hurt others because you have been hurt will only accomplish one thing: a tab to pick up later.

Compassion: Here is the word that will give you the true test that your healing process is working. You will have compassion that surpasses all understanding for others that are going through the same brokenness in their heart. The situation may be different, but your compassion and understanding will bring strength, ability to listen and feel their pain. You will begin to see a light of true healing in yourself, embracing the changes and transformation that are taking place day by day. You are starting to feel again.

_____

_____

_____

_____

_____

_____

_____

_____

_____

_____

Rule 11: What soap does for the body, tears do for the soul; a good tear bath works wonders.

Tears to fill a river: "What does this mean?" you may be asking yourself. Your tears will clean your soul, and the river will wash them away. Visualize a river flowing, and make the surroundings beautiful in your mind—a peaceful place to rest and heal. Let go, and let God heal your heart and repair the damage. Your faith will build, and you can rest assured that the Lord will carry you through. Crying is very good, but always shed your tears in a safe place. Many times people will not understand your pain, and your tears will push them away from you. Then there are some people that care about you a lot, and they think that talking about the situation and keeping it alive for years will help you. They don't realize it will only keep you in a mental prison and hinder your growth. Life is too precious to waste on the past.

_____

_____

_____

_____

_____

_____

_____

_____

_____

_____

Rule 12: Your worst enemy may not be a person but a choice.

No vices: OK! Get ready for the biggest news since plastic diapers: the vices you choose may be your worst enemy. Before I get into this section, clear your mind! The truth hurts, and denial is deadly. I believe in laying it out on the table and confronting the problem whatever it may be! "What is a vice?" you may be wondering.

- Cigarettes
- Alcohol
- Drugs
- Eating disorders
- Sex with people you don't even know
- Bad language
- Gossip
- Blaming other people
- Spending money you don't have
- Self-obsession

These are the top ten in the list of vices, and yes, there are many, many more to consider. You may not be participating in any of these, but these are for the record. When wanting to make a change in your life, you must clean all areas of your life or the bad things will get you back in the same mess you were in before. It may not be easy, but it will be worth it. This cleansing away of vices will give you respect for yourself and others. This is also the beginning of setting boundaries. No more being a prisoner to this list of harmful vices. If you are not able to cleanse from any of these by yourself, you may need help from someone who specializes in this process. There is help if you want it, but you have to make the choice. If you choose not to, you and only you stand in your way.

_____

_____

_____

_____

_____

_____

_____

_____

_____

_____

Rule 13: The truth sets us free! Lies will always catch up to the liar.

Don't curse others or yourself: These are words of wisdom. The whole process will waste your precious energy. When such thoughts cross your mind, close your eyes. Say the Serenity prayer that goes like this:

God grant me the Serenity to accept the things that I cannot change. The Courage to change the things I can, and the Wisdom to know the difference.

This prayer will help you clear your mind so the desire to curse others or yourself will be neutralized, even if you have to say it twenty times twenty.

When I talk about cursing yourself, it means don't speak negative things over your life. Like saying you are stupid, for example. You must reprogram every area of your life. Your words are powerful, and the use of daily negative words upon yourself or others is not a healthy environment for anyone. On the other hand, daily positive words can heal your soul and remove the pain from your heart. Saying positive affirmations will also help you to forgive. When you feel good about yourself, you can let go of the past and move forward to a new beginning.

I hope that you are smiling right now because this works if you just do it.

_____
_____
_____
_____
_____
_____
_____
_____
_____
_____

Rule 14: Look, learn, listen.

Says nothing about talking!

Be still, bridle your tongue, learn to listen: Well, congratulations! You have reached word 13 of the repair section of RR&R. Because this is last on the list, it is so important to digest these words and make them part of who you are.

Learn to *be still;* it takes great patience to learn this skill. It is a spiritual awakening that brings peace and joy back to your life. This small still voice will give you a newborn confidence in your faith.

Bridle your tongue will bring so much wisdom to your life. Think before you speak; don't just say things just to hear yourself talk.

Learn to listen will enrich your life with much success. Being a good listener is a wonderful gift; it will bring focus, clarity, and understanding. That is why God gave us two ears and one mouth because we need to listen. You will experience a whole new way of viewing life through listening. During this healing period, these wonderful words of wisdom will make such a dramatic change in your life that people around you will wonder what happened to the brokenness and want to know your secret. Just tell them that you are just *listening to your heart.*

Restore

Section 2 of the RR&R is *restore*. This section will meet you head on, developing and creating the new you. Once you get a handle on repairing your heart, you are ready to restore.

A *ccording to Webster, restore means to "return to former state or give back."* What's important to see in this definition is, number one, to return to former state, to take back or give back what has been taken. Finding your true self, being true to who you are, and transforming what is broken.

Here is your next list of seven words and seven rules that need your attention:

- Respect
- Appearance
- Goals
- Passion
- Relationships
- Home
- Hobbies

Rule 1:   Enough is enough.

Respect is earned, not just given. It is extremely important to respect yourself. Without respect, you will make poor choices for your life, allowing people to come into your life that are not good for you. Respect will also walk hand in hand with boundaries.

Once you build respect for yourself, you will graciously begin to show respect for others with, of course, boundaries.

_____

_____

_____

_____

_____

_____

_____

_____

_____

_____

Rule 2: Before looking at the eyelash in your brother's eye, check out the 2x4 in your own eye.

Appearance works hand in hand with respect for self.

This is a very important change that must take place in your healing process. Changing your appearance and reinventing yourself is the beginning of a new season in your life.

Your appearance will change the way you feel about yourself. Without saying a word, people will know how you feel by the way you dress and carry yourself. Take time out daily to do something nice for you. Respect for yourself will help you choose a classic style that will suit you. Having boundaries and respect in what you will allow yourself to wear in public says a lot about who you are as a person. When you start overexposing yourself for attention, you will draw the wrong attention. If you want to attract someone special in your life, make a positive change in your appearance. Do a little research, find out what you like, and see if the style works for you. Not every body type can wear the same styles. Wear what looks good on you; don't be pressured to wear what is trendy. Trendy does not work for all body types. You can never go wrong with a classic style.

Later in this book we will give more details about changing your style and appearance.

_____

_____

_____

_____

_____

_____

_____

_____

_____

_____

Rule 3:   If you can dream it, you can achieve it!

Goals are your road map with a GPS on your daily journey. Goals can be changed, but it is important to set some goals.

Don't be afraid to dream *big*! Write it all down, then you can set daily, monthly, and yearly goals. Set personal, spiritual, work, health, financial goals, and don't forget hobbies that you love to do but are always putting on the back burner. You will have to take a new inventory of what is important.

_____
_____
_____
_____
_____
_____
_____
_____
_____
_____
_____

Rule 4: Live, love, and laugh with passion.

Passion is a wonderful word. Once you allow passion into your life in all that you do, you will never be the same.

According to Webster, passion means "strong feelings or emotion; love especially sexual desire; anger, rage; the passion and sufferings of Christ."

Desire passion with your work, your time, and the way you love your family. Passion is a gift that forms in your heart to escalate your desire to enjoy even the simplest joys of life. Passion will burn like a fire in your soul that only can be removed if you don't desire it. God will allow the way when it looks like there is no way. This fire of passion will teach you to be grateful, thankful, full of prayer, joy, peace, singing, and dancing and will consume your being. So desire passion for your life, and restore the fire.

_____

_____

_____

_____

_____

_____

_____

_____

_____

_____

Rule 5: Choose your friends carefully!

Relationships need to be restored, which does not necessarily mean having the same people in your life.

This is a big one; due to the breakup, many people that you thought were your friends may not be there for you now. It's hard to accept this truth, that people that you daily broke bread with, went on vacations with, and created wonderful memories with are no longer in your life. It is truly sad, but you know what, there are new friends on your horizon. I hope you are smiling right now!

God has a plan, and once you take some time for yourself, put your ducks in a row—meaning get organized in your mind, body, and spirit—then the perfect timing will come for you to start making new friends. There is a sea of people out there that needs someone like you, once you have made the steps to let go of your past and look at your future as a new journey. When you know that you have something to bring to the table, not just your pain and story but a new, exciting special person that has something to give.

Not only will you be blessed, but you will be a blessing.

Rule 5 says it all: choose your friends carefully!

Test the waters; don't just jump into a shark tank and think that they are not hungry. Know that you are being tested, just as you will be testing your new relationships. Don't be afraid to say no and stand firm with your boundaries with new relationships. Remember you are worth more than just a test-drive. You are the showroom model, and you are not available to be test-driven. Your quality and wisdom should speak loudly. Always remember the apples at the top of the tree are the best. The fallen ones are broken and overripe. You are now on the vine; protect yourself from relationships that just want to eat you up and discard you. You are worth more than that.

_____

_____

_____

_____

_____

_____

_____

_____

_____

_____

Rule 6: Home is where your heart is!

Home is a special place that represents how you feel about you. Home can be a mirror that reflects your pain, peace, or joy. Being unorganized and having clutter everywhere will cloud your focus and cause confusion. It's time for a spring-cleaning.

Start with your bedroom. Your bedroom should be a beautiful place where you lay your head and sleep, a wonderful place of peace and serenity. Start by changing your bedspread and sheets to something special, and maybe, add more pillows. Your bedroom should be your safe place to heal.

Painting the walls a new color is a great start, or changing the pictures around you can give you new, creative ideas. Buy a new doormat, and add some houseplants or flowers inside and out.

FYI: If plants or flowers die, please throw them away, and get new ones. Having dead plants around does not bring good energy.

Having live plants gives you something to care for and something to take your mind off you. This helps you learn how to care for something that needs you. Animals are also good, but you must be ready for this responsibility. Animals don't deserve to be mistreated, so until you know that you are ready for the task of being a care provider, just stick to plants and flowers.

Open your windows, and let fresh air into your home every day if you can. Play your favorite music, sing and dance, and give thanks for this new beginning. Next, create a place where you can pray, write, and read daily. This will refresh and restore you spirit, mind, and body. Remember, your home is where your heart is, and when your heart is full of peace, you are at home.

Rule 7: Find what you love to do, and do it with passion!

Hobbies are creating activities out of spare time. This is plural; it's OK to have more than one hobby. If you don't have a hobby, it's time to find something that you love to do that allows you to express yourself. It's important that you have a physical hobby, which means to use your body—riding bikes, golf, yoga, dancing, etc.

A spiritual hobby means getting in tune with God—reading, meditation, praise and worship, writing, etc.

A mental hobby explores your creative side—drawing, painting, doing things with your hands, puzzles, chess, poker, something that makes you think.

Start by doing something that really makes you happy; start with one hobby, then add another. Hobbies don't have to cost money to do; singing and dancing in the kitchen could be the beginning of the dancing chef.

Hobbies are like good friends, and you often find great friends when you are doing your hobby. Always keep things in balance meaning don't let your hobby control your life. Also find hobbies that make you get outside or do something other than being on your computer or watching television. Design, create, express yourself, pray, sing, dance, and fill your spirit with joy and happiness. It's very easy to do—just do it!

Reclaim

S ection 3 of RR&R is *reclaim*; this section is powerful and has the ability to transform the renewing of your mind and give you hope and peace that surpasses all understanding. With this amazing opportunity, you can move mountains with the wisdom that you now possess. At this stage, you have addressed many issues and have felt the pulling of your heartstrings beginning to move into position like a fine-tuned instrument. These last five words deal with you and the choices that you are about to make. The choices that you make will come with some form of action, and once you take the action, there is always a tab to pick up, either positive or negative. Either way, both will possess a life lesson that will give you wisdom. I pray that you will find the strength to always make the right choice. Though sometimes very hard, always remember, when in doubt, do the right thing. When you don't know what to say, say the kind thing. If you get in trouble, always tell the truth.

According to Webster, reclaim means "make usable, make reusable, redeem from vice."

Here are the last five words that need your attention of RR&R. Embrace them, and be free from your pain; tomorrow is just a sunrise away.

- Dreams
- Commitment
- Integrity
- Moral courage
- Change

Rule 1:   Don't look back; look into your future with passion!

Dreams open our lives to faith and hope. Don't waste your time looking at yesterday when today is full of exciting opportunities, and tomorrow's sunrise will be waiting for you in the eastern sky; all you have to do is get up and watch for this extraordinary gift.

God is always talking to us through our dreams and visions, through the music we hear, and through the people we meet or birds that fly and babies that laugh or cry. There are always messages if we just listen. There are always unique signals seeking our attention. It's what our dreams are made of, signs from the Almighty God charting a path to the course that will bring us to our destiny.

Write down your dreams; there is often a message that will have a life lesson that can help you when you don't know what to do. Remember to ask God for guidance when you don't understand a dream. He will give you understanding; just don't take action without prayer. Dreams can often hold a warning or an answer to prayer, so don't ignore your dreams.

Rule 2:   Remember, your *yes* means *yes,* and your *no* means **no***!*

Commitment, commitment, commitment!

When you commit to someone or something, you must follow through. You should always think about it before you answer; let your *yes* be *yes* and your *no* be *no!* No more jumping into the shallow end of the pool headfirst; if you do, it could hurt you very badly. Don't sit on the fence and ponder; there is no room to play games in any area of your life; it's a waste of your time. Once you have committed to someone or something, there is *no* backing out. (There are very few cases that you should back out, and it should only be for an extreme emergency; no lying!) At this point, you have done a lot of work on yourself; the worst thing to do is fall into old habits. Habits are not hobbies, and if you have a few habits that you treat like hobbies, get rid of them *now*!

What happened in your last relationship stemmed from a broken commitment. Make sure that when you trust someone with your heart that you know that they understand what this word means; don't just give it away to someone who does not have a clue, or you will be back in the same boat without a paddle. Or worse, be on a horse without a saddle; if you have ever ridden a horse without a saddle, you get the picture: pain in the first degree.

Commit with integrity.

_____

_____

_____

_____

_____

_____

_____

_____

_____

_____

Rule 3:   What speaks louder than words is a person with integrity.

According to Webster, integrity means "intactness, firmness of character, honesty, etc."

Integrity forms the very fiber of a person's character. Integrity defines who we are as a person, what we are made of when it comes to dealing with all issues in our lives. Without integrity, we will not stand in a storm; we will set the sails on our boat to low and miss the wind every time. Integrity is the wind beneath our sails that will keep us on the right path.

You must dig deep and stand on your convictions with integrity; don't bend just to please another. Because in the end, people will let you down, and you will have lost your integrity. Reclaim what is yours; your integrity is who you are.

_____

_____

_____

_____

_____

_____

_____

_____

_____

_____

Rule 4: Hearing the truth sets you free; standing on the truth keeps you humble.

Moral courage is a form of courage that very few people possess. It takes integrity to stand with moral courage. It basically means having principles with bravery. Often in our lives, we may witness a situation where someone has done something, and we turn the other way due to not wanting to get involved.

In a relationship, moral courage gets involved when you know that the other person who has committed to you decides that it would be best to dissolve the relationship. It's important to use your moral courage to make that person accountable for what he or she is doing. It could be cheating, lying, stealing, etc. Don't stand by and let bad actions harm you and others. If this person continues getting away with harming others, more innocent people will get hurt until someone calls them on their bad actions. Find your moral courage, and make a stand.

As we draw to the end of RR&R, these last five words for reclaiming your life bring all the lessons home. A full circle of healing is taking place.

_____

_____

_____

_____

_____

_____

_____

_____

_____

_____

Rule 5:   As the road comes to the end, you must choose to make a turn in a new direction.

Change is such a wonderful word with endless opportunities; it all depends on which direction you decide to take, and the choice is yours. When you understand that every heartache comes with a life lesson that can be used for your good, if you reclaim and make the change to look forward into your future and leave your past in the past. Change the way you talk about yourself, and you will be able to change the way you think about those that have harmed you. It all begins with you. Nothing can rob you of your sense of purpose but you!

Time can change you, but you can't change time or the past.

Turn in a new direction, and possess what is yours. Change is not always easy; review what you have learned, and each day, you will get stronger, and then one day, when you rise early in the morning to catch that sunrise, you will know that something good is going to happen today because you are alive and you have purpose.

Perseverance, Patience, and Prayer

Perseverance means to "persist in spite of obstacles."

Patience means "enduring without complaint."

Prayer means to "ask earnestly for, petition or worship a divinity."

These words have such wisdom, such strength in their definition, truly a treasure to behold. Take each of these words, and make them your own. Like a seed, bury them deep into the soil of your heart. Say these words to yourself like an affirmation, using the definitions with the word and add "I will." Your inner strength will begin to awaken, and you will be able to make the changes that need to happen.

Be sure to write out your thoughts in this book like a journal. You will be able to look back on your progress in a few weeks and see how you have grown spiritually, mentally, and physically. You will also love the way you look and the new way you listen and speak to others. Just take one day at a time and know that "time can change you, but you can't change time." Embrace the life lessons, and celebrate the wisdom that you have gained.

Boundaries

This is one of the most important sections of this book: creating boundaries. Life without boundaries is like a boat with no bottom. Without boundaries in our lives, we don't make good choices, and we have a tendency to run amok. Of course, our picker becomes broken, and we allow people and things into our life that we need to let go of; they are called the nowhere people. They don't know where they are going, and they want you to stay with them, and if you don't know what a picker is, it's the person making the decisions in your life, which in most cases will be yourself.

The first step in creating boundaries is to learn how to say *no*! When you start putting boundaries around your life, some people are not going to like the new changes that are happening. They are used to you just going along with whatever; well, whatever is not good enough. Whatever will get you in places you don't need or want to be in; also, when you begin to put up boundaries, you will be tested, just to make sure you really mean what you meant to do. What is exciting about this process is once you see the true benefits, you will start to attract really amazing people in your life. Boundaries work in *all* areas of your life, not just some. Here are a few examples of boundaries; these suggestions will be life changing:

■ VICES create stumbling blocks in your life. A sewer full of some of the worst enemies that you could allow into your life could be sitting on your coffee table or in your closet. We are told they calm our nerves, help with stress, etc. But the truth is they are killing you inside, taking years, robbing you of your health. Until you lose your good health, only then will you understand the consequence that you have allowed in your life. Choosing not to have vices in your life will be the first step to true freedom. Vices keep you prisoner, and the only person that has the key to release you is you!

■ RELATIONSHIPS should not cause pain. When you are thinking about getting into a relationship and start spending time with someone special, make sure they are bringing good things to the table. If they have vices, complain all the time, are late, curse, speak poorly about others, lack integrity, have money problems, no belief system, just to name a few, please, please measure the work that you are doing in your life to repair the brokenness. Take a long look in the mirror at yourself before you enter into a new relationship. You deserve to be happy; don't just jump into another relationship just because you feel lonely.

■ SEX should always come with boundaries, especially if you are not married. Having sex before marriage puts you on a different playing field. Having sex when you are just dating does not promise you that the other person is going to commit to you only. Sex does not buy you love nor does it mean love; some people think because they have sex with someone they are now a couple, which means commitment. Well, big news flash, not in today's world. Please don't give yourself away to someone that does not love you or care enough about you to wait. Being a virgin is a gift from God; once you give it away, there is no way to get it back. Some people will make fun of you for being a virgin; purity is not a joke, it is a gift. Protect your gift, and don't let anyone take that from you; it is truly special. If you are not a virgin and have been married or in a relationship where you have given your virginity away, it is not too late to have boundaries. Honor yourself, and don't just give yourself away like the past. Put up your boundaries, and you will see that you are better than just a free test-drive. Remember, people want what they can't have. Take a stand, put up your boundaries, and you will be glad that you did. Here is one more suggestion to help you walk this walk of having sex in a relationship or before marriage: think about giving yourself a purity ring, bracelet, or necklace as a promise to being true to yourself. Look on the Internet, and learn more about this subject. It is very eye-opening. When you have a boundary over your own body, you will begin to understand that it is a gift to share with your soul mate and not just a one-night stand.

■ FRIENDS are special people; choose your friends carefully. A friend should want the best for you, not be jealous of you, will be there through the good times and the bad. They will not be judgmental, but they will always tell you the truth even if it means losing you as a friend. Sometimes, friends come into your life for a season at a time. They go away, but later in life, they find their way back onto your path. That means you both needed to grow. Sometimes, you have to weed your friends like a garden for your own growth; if not, you will never follow your dreams or leave your comfort zone. Friends are rare treasures; don't settle for imitations.

■ MONEY can create many opporunities, but when it creates friends, you need to take a long look in the mirror. Do your new friends like you or your money? It is so awesome to be able to give to others and share your financial success. But when it comes to friends, relationships, sex, vices, jobs, clothes, entertainment, belief system, etc., you really need to have boundaries, and if you don't, two things will happen. Either you will become an egomaniac and abuse people, or people will begin to abuse you. Having the finances to do what you want is great, but use it for your good. Lay down a solid foundation of how you spend your money, and have boundaries. Money can make you feel like you are special, and people will treat you differently, but it does not mean that it is real. If you are coming out of a relationship and you have been given a settlement, you need to know that people are going to come out of the woodwork at you. Choose your friends carefully, and be very careful who you let into your life. Put up the boundaries, and protect yourself in all areas; this includes family and friends. Be true to yourself, and always live your life with a sense of purpose; if not, you will end your days with much regret. Every person has their price; don't use your money for evil. Temptation is real; don't use your money to make people stumble. It will be just a tab you have to pick up later. Money is not the root to all evil; it's what you do with the money that creates an action that creates the root.

■ JOBS are not easy to find if you're not sure what you want to do, but you know you need money. You have got to first put up boundaries of what you are willing and not willing to do. Selling yourself out and doing something that will harm your life is not wise but stupid. Looking for someone to take care of you is not a job; don't even go there. Letting someone else pay your bills will only rob you of your dreams. Being able to provide for yourself is not only humbling but makes you have confidence and gives you strength to endure life's challenges. You will not gain that strength having a sugar daddy or sugar mommy; when you depend on those people, they can throw you out on your bum, then where will you be? Set your goals, and do some research of what your interests are, then go to school or get a job, even if you have to rough it for a year. It will be worth it. Do not let vices or nowhere people into your life when it comes to looking for work. Set your goals for one month, three months, six months, and then one year. Then it will be time to ask in prayer for your dream job. Don't be afraid to ask in prayer; it has a miraculous working power.

■ CLOTHES are an extension of who you are, but don't become a slave to fashion. Finding a style that fits your personality and body type is gratifying. Looking for clothes that fit your body can be very challenging; if you are trying to fit your body into clothes that don't fit your body shape, it's even more challenging. So many women and men are fashion slaves, and in many cases, they look silly wearing low-cut jeans or skinny jeans that don't suit their bodies or trying to dress like a model in a magazine. Example, the model is five feet ten inches and wears a size 6, and you're five feet six inches and a size 6, and you are wondering why the outfit does not look the same. There is a height difference that changes everything. Choose what looks good on you; you will be a lot happier creating your own style. You may be asking why I do have to have boundaries with my clothes. Boundaries are all about not crossing a line, having limits, knowing when to say no, and knowing when your clothes are too short, too low, too see-through, too tight, etc. The way we dress represents who we are and how we feel about ourselves. I admire designers for their designs, but they don't often design for the mainstream man or woman. They design for one body type; it's all about the runway and the show. These are the fashions you see in magazines. Draw your line in the sand, and think about who you are, what makes you feel beautiful, something that does not fit you properly, or the perfect fit that turns heads. Thank God there are many designers, and we don't have to all wear the same thing. When you are reinventing yourself, you must take into account how you dress. Reinventing does not mean wearing less clothes; it does mean finding your style. So many women and men go in the wrong direction when coming out of a breakup, thinking that someone will think they are hot, sexy, trendy, and stylish in something that is very revealing or overexposing themselves. You will attract the wrong kind of person if you put yourself out there like that. Showing all that you have does nothing but limits your opportunities. But of course, it does depend on what opportunities you are interested in. If you want quality, dress like you are quality. More doors will open for you. Boundaries will help you make the right decisions; test it for yourself.

■ ENTERTAINMENT should be entertaining. But enough is enough. Everything has sexual undertones or cursing; there is absolutely nothing left for the imagination. Movies, games, music expose so much that it's just not entertaining. It's shocking but not entertaining. Sports is about the only safe thing to watch nowadays, but of course, there are a few exceptions in that arena. It is so important to be careful what you put in your eyes and ears. When you are going through a breakup, the last thing you need is negative images and sounds playing in your head. Once again, you must protect yourself with boundaries, but only you can make that decision. If not, you will harden your heart and become numb to what is around you. Some people may give you a hard time in the beginning, but take a stand. Stay strong to your convictions, be an example, and you will be surprised what a transformation you will experience. Putting positive, pure thoughts in your head brings a true sense of self and purpose. You may be thinking that with all these boundaries, you are not going to have fun. I promise that when you make these changes you are going to start enjoying life more than ever. Instead of watching girls running around with no clothes and people saying, "F this and F that," go watch the sunset, or better yet, watch a sunrise. Get up early in the morning and just go meditate or read. Cook something special, and listen to some amazing guitar, piano, or violin music. Take a bubble bath, start painting, take ballroom dance classes, two-step, hip-hop, tap, fencing, learn another language, fly a helicopter. The world is full of fun, exciting, entertaining things to do, but you have to put up some boundaries and go live.

BELIEF system is the root to all that is good. Once you start making changes and creating boundaries, your life is going to become so exciting. You are going to birth such confidence in your spirit that you are going to look back in a few months and say to yourself, "What was I thinking! Why did I think so little of myself to allow such things in my life?" Getting in tune with your spiritual life will help you strengthen your faith; life without faith is empty.

"With God, all things are possible" (Matthew 19:26). This verse says it all. Having a belief system and living your life with a true sense of purpose will bring such joy and peace to your life that surpasses all understanding. Everything in life is not easy to understand, but with faith, it gives you the courage to press on and the strength to endure the trials that cross your path. This is another process that will have some people making fun of you or questioning your motivation. Stand strong, choose your words carefully, and walk away. Believe me, I have walked this path of ridicule from many people that I thought were my friends, but as time passed, each one of them slowly in their own time got on the same path. No words can truly describe the amazing transformation that occurs in one's life once you have found the truth.

Irrational Things

After a breakup, we can do some pretty irrational things; here are a few ideas of what not to do. Remember, people want what they can't have. When you understand this theory, you will soon see how things change in your life:

"Can we talk? I'm begging you."

Wipe your tears, and walk away with dignity! Begging someone that wants to leave a relationship that has already made up their mind to leave just puts more fuel on the fire and more arrows in your heart. Begging only makes them feel powerful over you, and they will begin to abuse you. As much as it hurts, you must let go. Begging someone to love you or to stay goes nowhere.

Computer Love vs. Computer Spy

In today's world of technology, it is hard to hide from the pain of a breakup where you can text, IM, e-mail, social network yourself into a world of despair if you are not careful. Seeing your ex move into the single market is hard when you are still emotional about the breakup. Being able to monitor their every move is not the path you want to travel. Spying on them will only make you crazy and make you feel desperate. Sending love messages will only make you look like a stalker. Don't let your emotions send you over the edge. "Time can change you, but you can't change time." Give yourself time to heal, grieve, and you will be glad you did. Having regrets later in life for the stupid things you did in the name of love is truly a life lesson. There is no shame in love; the shame or regret is being with someone that does not deserve you. You deserve more, but you must be true to yourself. Don't chase what was; chase what's in your future, not your past.

Breakup Sex Leads to Making Up—or Does It?

This is the hardest area to give advice about. Every situation is different, but the one common bond is there has been a breakup. We all know there's a period of time after a breakup where sex with your ex is going to happen. It's only natural for you to still want to be physical with someone that you have loved, and you're trying to save that relationship. But if it's been at least six months after your breakup, and there is no sign of a reunion or makeup, then there is a real problem that needs to be dealt with. If not, someone is going to get their heart broken beyond measure. Allowing someone that does not love you or will not commit to you to use you for sex is *not* acceptable. It does not matter about your history with this person, let go! There will be no makeup with this breakup; it's time to wake up.

Let's Be Friends

This is an easy one to give advice about; the answer is *no*! The question should be *why*? If you have children together, then yes, you should be friends in a kind way for the sake of your children. But if you are just trying to be friends so you can hang out together with other people, you are heading in the wrong direction. Let go! You can be friends later in life, but at this moment, get on another path, start doing new things, and don't show up at parties or places where you know your ex will be. Because if you still have feelings for your ex, you are going to put yourself in a terrible position where you will be the one out of line. If you are still in school and you have to see this person daily, be kind, get busy, stay focused, and make new friends.

Seeing your ex with another is not easy, so don't put yourself through the pain. It will cause resentment and rob you of your peace.

QUESTIONS TO THINK ABOUT

There are no right or wrong answers, but you must be true to yourself. Use this book to dig deep inside and learn from your pain. For some people, it takes several times to learn a lesson. The only problem with repeating the lesson over and over again is you're wasting valuable time that you don't get back. Writing down your thoughts has a way of permeating your heart and healing the wounds inside. Please take your time and read the questions aloud; answer them honestly, but think before you write. This is a good way to learn how to listen before you answer.

Q: If tomorrow never comes, will you have done the things you wanted and needed to do? If not, make a list.

Q: Will you have said what you needed to say? If not, say it now, and write it down even if you have to go get a notebook.

_____
_____
_____
_____
_____
_____
_____
_____
_____
_____

Q: Will you have loved? If you are reading this book, your answer should be yes; if it is no, then you will want to continue reading.

Q: Have you forgiven those that hurt you or disappointed you? If yes, you've made awesome progress. If no, why? Write it down.

_____

_____

_____

_____

_____

_____

_____

_____

_____

_____

WHEN THE BREAKUP HAS NO MAKEUP, IT IS TIME TO WAKE UP!

Q: Do or will you have regrets? Write them down.

Q: Who is your closest friend? Why?

_____

_____

_____

_____

_____

_____

_____

_____

_____

_____

Q: What do you miss most about your ex? Write it down.

Q: Now that the healing process has begun, will you let go of the past and move on? If not, why? Write it down.

_____
_____
_____
_____
_____
_____
_____
_____
_____
_____
_____

Q: Knowing how badly your heart was broken, if you went to the mall, gym, etc., and met this amazing person, would you jump into a new relationship? Yes? No? Why? Write it down.

Once you go through the healing process, you are ready to start dating again. One day, you run into this amazing person, you start talking, and you find out that they have just broken up with someone.

Q: Would you start dating them, or would you suggest that they spend some time going through the process of healing? Write it down.

_____

_____

_____

_____

_____

_____

_____

_____

_____

_____

Q: Your best friend is going through a divorce. What advice would you give them? Write it down.

Q: After your healing process, one year goes by, and you run into your ex; you're looking great and feeling better than ever. Your ex wants to go out; you are available. What would you do? Write it down.

_____
_____
_____
_____
_____
_____
_____
_____
_____
_____

Q: After your healing process, one year goes by, and you run into your ex with their date. You look great and feel awesome. What do you do? If they come over to you, what do you do? Write it down.

Q: What five awesome treasures of wisdom have you taken from this book? Write it down.

_____

_____

_____

_____

_____

_____

_____

_____

_____

_____

Reinventing the New You!

In this chapter, we are going to address steps to reinventing the new you! You may be saying "I like the old me," and that's great; you don't have to change a thing. If you have gotten to this page in the book and you are loving the way you look and feel, then awesome!

But if you find yourself at this page and want a few ideas for some little changes, keep reading. I will touch base and give some simple but effective tips on a few of the oblivious areas that you can address.

Since you've done so much work on the inside, it's time to do a little work on the outside.

Hair

Let's start with hair. What is so great about hair is you can cut it off, and within a few months, it's long again. You can try so many styles, cuts, and colors, but the important part is finding what looks good on you. Before you do anything, first get your hair into great condition. If you have long hair, short hair, or curly hair, note that any hair that's dry, stringy, and lacks shine is not attractive. Use products that are going to give your hair body and shine. Get your ends trimmed every six to eight weeks to maintain beautiful long hair and every three to four weeks for short hair to maintain your style.

Let's Talk Color

Once you get your hair in great condition, it's time to talk about hair color choices. There are rainbows of colors you can choose from; what's important is to consider what will look good on you. Highlights are not for everybody; let me give you an example of one of my clients. Maggie came to me as a new client with salt-and-pepper hair; her skin is very tan because she loves to be out in the sun. She was looking for a change and thought she would get some highlights. After we had a chance to talk, we decided on doing a beautiful dark red. Not only does Maggie look ten years younger, but she looks awesome. She had always been a brunette, so the transition was not hard due to her staying in the same color level, meaning she is a level 4 and her new color is a level 4. If she had chosen to have highlights, it would have washed her out. As she is today, she is vibrant and looks very natural.

If you really want highlights, find a hairstylist that you trust and ask them about your options. Highlights don't always have to be blond, but giving your hair depth and contrast is beautiful for long and short hair. Color will give your hair more body and luster, so giving your hair a color burst would be a very simple change that makes a huge difference.

Let's Talk Hairstyles

Hairstyles are such a personal choice; some people have awesome curly hair, but they want straight hair. Then of course, the people that have awesome straight hair want curly hair. Guess what? You can have both, just keep in mind the third paragraph of this section: keep your hair in good condition! Curling, rolling, and flatironing are so hard on the hair, so you must use good products to protect your hair during these processes.

Curly

If you want curly hair, you may want to try some old methods like sponge rollers—they come in lots of sizes—or maybe rag-set your hair. Take an old T-shirt and cut it into long strips, then twist the hair around the strips and tie in a soft knot. Hair can be slightly damp. Let dry while you sleep. Blow-dry each curl in the morning, and take them down. You will have amazing curls, or try curling your hair with bobby pins or clips. Tip: the smaller the section of hair, the curlier it will be. These ideas can be a fun way to make changes without spending a lot of money. Also you don't have to use so much heat on your hair, so your hair will stay in better condition.

Straight

If you want straight hair, it is best to blow-dry straight first, then use a flatiron. When you just use the flatiron, you are putting too much direct heat on the hair, and you could cause breakage. The best tip is to use a straightening gel/spray/cream during blow-drying to protect the hair; there are several really good brands on the market. Just ask your stylist. There are also chemical methods that are available, but most of them must be done by your stylist.

Styles

To create a new style, don't be afraid to change your part. You can always change it back. Wearing hair accessories is always a fun way to make a change. Wearing headbands or pulling your hair back in a high or low ponytail or braiding and twisting your hair are fun, simple, casual looks that just take a few minutes to do. Change does not mean it has to be hard.

Awesome Skin, Makeup, Brows, and More

There is nothing more beautiful than flawless skin!

Having flawless skin is a dream of mine. I have had the pleasure of working on some of the most beautiful women in the world, and yes, they have flawless skin—not all of them but most. The one common bond is they take care of their skin. They are committed to cleansing, moisturizing, and using sunscreen daily. They also drink lots of water. So with that said, finding the right product that works for your skin type is the key. Using a trendy product just because it's in a magazine is not always best for your skin type. As an example, I will use my own skin regimen for this section of skin care.

In my early teens and early twenties, I had really nice skin. I thought, *Great, I missed teenage acne*, then I decided to go on the pill. What a great idea—NOT!

For about two years my skin was pretty clear, but then I decided I did not need the pill and got off it. Well, let me tell you what happened; all that teenage acne came knocking on my face. The doctor told me to get back on the pill. I thought, *You have got to be kidding, what is happening to my body, what have I done?* As you may have gathered, I did not get back on the pill, but my product-testing days began. I have tested more products on my own face, looking for the perfect skin—care regimen for my skin type, and it has been an eye-opening experience. The good thing is I've learned a lot about products, so when my actors or clients come in and tell me what they are using, I know what to expect. Believe me, this was not my intention to become a product guru. What I did learn is that simple is better; going back to basic skin care works best. If you have the money to spend on pricey products, awesome, but if you are on a budget, believe me, you can find great products in a drugstore.

Don't let the trendy products make you feel like you have to spend a lot of money to have flawless skin because you don't.

Makeup!

What girl doesn't love makeup? Makeup is creative and is extremely helpful when you need to cover flaws. As a hair-and-makeup artist, I have been able to live out my dream of doing something I love: making people feel good about themselves and getting paid for it. Yea, me! I have been to the best schools, worked in the best cities for the  film and beauty industry. But I have to say some of my best makeup tips came from my mom. Call it old school, but she taught me things that I still use today in my work. The reason, I tell you this, is that our mothers will tell us the truth about the way we look. Sometimes even our closest friends will not tell us we are wearing too much lipstick or too much eye shadow, etc. But our moms will because they love us and don't want us to look bad. I have a motto in my business, and it goes like this: "We love to see the woman and not just her makeup."

What this means is when you wear too much makeup, people only see the mask, not the real you. When going through the process of reinventing yourself, you have many options to create a morning look, daytime look, and an evening look, and they can all be very different.

Morning look: can be just sunscreen, lip gloss, and a hint of mascara.
Daytime look: can be tinted moisturizer with sunscreen, lip gloss, mascara, and a hue of blush with a soft brown liner on your top eyelid.
Evening look: foundation, concealer, powder, blush, eye shadow, liner, mascara, eyebrow pencil, lipstick, and gloss.

More makeup does not mean it has to be really dark.

Finding a happy medium is the secret. When you see celebrities in magazines, they are not always wearing the red-carpet face. Most celebrities do not wear a lot of makeup when they are not working; they do wear moisturizer, sunscreen and take care of their skin.

Brows Are the Frame of the Eyes: Without Brows, Your Face Looks Naked

Brows

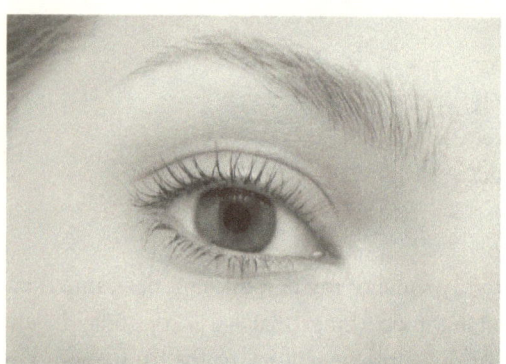

Brows have a way of showing expression and true elegance. Looking at Hollywood stars from the twenties to seventies, they had the most expressive eyes. They truly set the stage for all makeup trends as styles come and go. So do brows. But beautifully groomed brows are always in style. Filling in your brows with brow powder or pencil either way will work. It's what works for you, but filling them in will make a huge difference in your finished makeup application. When you have strong brows, you can wear less eye shadow. You can still line your eyes, but use less color. Do your own research; it's a lot of fun to see the different styles of brows throughout the years. It's quite the education.

Fragrance

With all the different beauty products to choose from, my favorite is fragrances; it is my weakness. I love fresh, clean smells from the clothes I wear, my hair, my home, and my car. I love fragrance!

I believe fragrances can really change your mood in a positive way. If you don't have a favorite fragrance, go do this for yourself and find that perfect scent. I want to tell you how I came to love perfumes so much. It started with my habit of cigarette smoking. I smoked for several years; as a smoker, I lost my taste buds and my sense of smell. I really could not smell anything; people would smell something really bad and ask me if I could smell it, and I would say no.

I tried to quit smoking several times, but I just wouldn't stick to the program. Most of my friends smoked, so I did too. My habit was so bad that I would wake up in the middle of the night just to smoke. Then something happened one night. It was very cold outside, and I went out to smoke on my patio. I began to shiver uncontrollably, and as I continued to smoke, I cried out to God, "Please help me stop smoking and release me from this prison." I had become a slave to cigarettes, and at that moment, I was done. Really done! As I walked inside, I started to dry my tears, and I felt this peace come over me, and I felt really tired. When I fell asleep, I slept so soundly the rest of the night, which I had not done in several years. When I got up, I got dressed and ate something and then I realized I had not had a cigarette. By that time in the morning, I would have had at least five or six, but I did not have an urge to smoke. At noon that day, I still did not want to smoke, but I lit up anyway, and it tasted terrible. Then I tried to smoke later that evening, and again, it tasted terrible. At that point, I knew God had heard my prayer, and I was *not* going to enjoy smoking ever again. I tried several more times, and each time just got worse; after that, I did not desire to smoke again. But the next thing that happened was my taste buds became alive, and my sense of smell became acute. It was like an old world where I had forgotten the smells and tastes. This was a miracle. Since I stopped smoking, I had all this extra money each month, so I decided to buy fragrances. From one vice to another, I became obsessed with perfumes, and I bought perfumes like I bought cigarettes. Then one day, I realized what I was doing and began to cry. I was in a prison again buying perfumes. I prayed again for self-control and wisdom. I believe that prayer works, and it is very important to be careful what you pray for because you just might get it.

God gave me self-control and wisdom that were absent from my life. I am so glad that he heard and answered my prayers. I still buy perfumes, but I do it with self-control.

Finding Your Style That Fits Your Body

When I began this section of reinventing myself, I found it extremely difficult. The reason why is that I have a style in my head of how I would love to dress. But when I go out shopping, I can't find it. Everything is either too young, like I am wearing my niece's clothes, or too old, like I am wearing my grandmother's clothes, too see-through, too tight, too short, does not fit my body type—it makes me want to scream. I want to dress femininely with a classic tailored look with comfort and style. I don't usually like trendy clothes, but I may buy one or two pieces a season if they work with some of my other outfits. I really love quality designs and fabrics, but the price tags are often too extreme for my budget. So I have learned to shop wisely!

When I shop, I look at it like a project: I'm the model, and I need to find that perfect outfit. When I use that mind-set, I usually find deals, but if I just go shopping aimlessly, most of the time I come home with nothing.

So in this section, I would love to help you in putting new looks together.

Undergarments

I had to start here because this is so important. Without the proper undergarments, that perfect dress or pants just don't look good. Even T-shirts look bad, but when you have a bra that fits and gives you the proper lift—look out, world.

It does not matter what your bra size is. It's the fit that matters, and that makes the difference. Try on different styles and brands until you find that perfect fit; it will be worth it.

Bras and panties are the perfect place to start in this process of reinventing yourself. When undergarments fit well, you feel good; if they are too tight or too loose, you feel uncomfortable. Finding undergarments with a tummy control works wonders no matter what your size is. These garments will give you a firmer and smoother look. So get started here first to find your perfect fit.

Finding Your Style

This is not always easy! Before you do anything, let's do a little spring-cleaning and see what you have to work with first. See what fits properly. Can you use it to layer? If you have not worn it in three years, give it away unless it is an heirloom. Some classic styles can be in style for years, so really look at what's in the closet.

Second, do a little research; look through magazines, catalogs, and Web sites; and look at fashions that you think would fit your body type. Then research brands/designers that carry styles that you like, and make sure that they make your size. Some designers make a size 6, but it fits like a size 4, so really research the designer. A suggestion that could really be fun is to create a research journal for hairstyles, makeup, clothes, etc. Cut pictures out, document the Web sites and designers and where you can find/buy them.

Next, think about the colors you love to wear. If you like bright colors, look for designers that make colorful clothes. Some designs work mainly with earth tones, so before you waste your time, do a little research on what you like.

Next, think about fabrics. There are so many fabrics, but some fabrics look great on some people, and on others, it's a train wreck. So find the fabrics that work for you so when you go shopping, you can look for those fabrics that work and steer clear of the ones that don't. Design for yourself a spring, summer, and fall fabric list. In some parts of the world, they have at least three seasons, some just two, but find what fabrics work for you for each season.

Now that you've cleaned out your closet, done your research, and located designers, stores, your style, color, and fabric, you are ready to go shopping.

Let's look at your budget and determine what you need most in your wardrobe. Sometimes, just adding a scarf or belt to an outfit can really bring the look together and can look like a new outfit. Scarves are a big favorite of mine year-round. In the winter, they really keep you warm; in summer, they can protect your skin. Draping linen or cotton scarves around your shoulders in the summer is a great look and will keep you cool. If you get too hot, just wrap it around your waist. Create your own trademark style with scarves.

Adding jackets to any skirt, jeans, or pants is always a great look. Having a short blue-jean jacket in your wardrobe is a great casual classic. You can dress it up or down. A black or navy tailored jacket is also a must-have in your closet; classic yet you can dress it up or down. By adding accessories, you can create several different looks with these two jackets.

The little black dress is also a classic. Using scarves, accessories, belts, different shoes, or jackets can make that little black dress look like several new outfits very easily.

Jeans are a great American fashion style. Over the years, designers have taken blue jeans that used to be clothes that you worked in the fields and mines and made them a high fashion statement. Jeans are a must-have in your closet if they fit your body type and style. Jeans don't look good on every body type, so don't feel forced to follow a fashion trend. If you look better in dresses, linen pants, skirts, etc., wear what looks good on you. You will be happier and make a better impression with the people you meet. Be true to yourself.

Wearing clothes that don't fit properly—being too big or too tight—does not make a good impression about who you are. Pulling up your clothes and not being able to sit because your pants are too tight, too big, or too small is not a smart way to leave your home every day. Believe it or not, you can cause health issues by wearing your clothes too tight; this is for both women and men. It is something to think about.

On wearing clothes that expose too much of your body, if you are going swimming, then make sure you have the body to wear a bikini. Be sure to use sunscreen, and enjoy yourself. Always think about the people around you. If you have a hot, smoking, rock-hard body, you have done a lot of work on yourself and are proud of your accomplishment, but if children are in your area, please have enough respect for those kids—don't overexpose yourself. Put a beautiful scarf around your bum and breast and know that you will earn more respect from other women and men than you could ever imagine. Always remember, there will always be a tab to pick up even when it seems so innocent as to be lying in your bikini at the beach or a pool.

People are always watching; you never know when you will need someone to watch your back, and if you put yourself out there in a negative way that harms others, you may be setting yourself up to a rude awakening. These are words of wisdom that I share with you, and this is just one example of being kind to others. If you have children, you will understand this example; if you don't have children, it may be harder for you to understand the damage that one can cause by being self-obsessed. This example also relates to wearing street clothes that are too tight or overexposing yourself for attention.

New example: you are walking down the street with your tight skirt and buttoned-up blouse and heels. You work in an office and walk to lunch; you have a jacket, but you leave it in the office. You are a professional and have worked hard to earn your position at work. On your way to lunch, there is a construction site that you walk by. As you get to the middle of the site, the men are at lunch. They see you and start the catcalls. You think *Those j—s* or you think *What a bunch of sweet guys.* Some of the catcalls are crude and get you upset. You get back to the office and wonder, *What did I do to get that kind of treatment?* First, your *short* tight skirt, your buttoned-up blouse is exposing your *cleavage* and is *see-through,* and your high heels scream *stripper.* The point that I am making is that people are always watching other people; if you want respect, you must dress with respect. What you wear to a nightclub is not acceptable to wear at work. The sad thing is, no one in your office is telling you to your face that you are exposing yourself. But be assured that behind your back, they have many feelings about the way you dress. This example may not relate to you, but you may know someone that fits this description. If you are not able to tell them without being fired or getting into a verbal battle (*word battle* sounds better than *fight*), just give them a copy of this book and let them read this chapter. Who knows, they may see clearly to change their ways.

We Are What We Eat!

This little statement says it all: we are what we eat! It's very important when we are going through a breakup that we take care of ourselves. It's sad but true; we either lose a lot of weight or gain a lot of weight. Breaking up is not a fun venture; you have to look at it as a life experience that came with a lot of adventure that ended with an eating disorder. With that said, once you have gone through the fire of the breakup and you are ready to wake up, you can look at yourself and see that it's time to make a change in your eating habits. Whether it's losing too much weight or gaining too much, it's time to reinvent the old you.

For me, I was a size 10 and dropped to a size 6. It was not my intention to lose weight. But I had no appetite, and the weight just kept falling off. Then I had a closet full of clothes that didn't fit me. Some people would call this a quality problem, but I am tall and don't want to look that thin. Plus I like to cook and eat, so I realized after almost a year, it's time to start enjoying life again.

Here are a few questions to ponder on:

Q: When we try to lose weight, how come the weight does not drop off as easily?

My guess: I think the weight stays on because we are concentrating so much on trying to lose weight that our metabolism just shuts down. On the other hand, I think our metabolism feels our pain and starts to work in overdrive so we lose weight, or it says, "I love chocolate anytime," so we knock ourselves out then we gain weight.

Q: Do you eat to live or live to eat?

My guess: To maintain a healthy body is to eat to live. When we live to eat, we may have a tendency to overindulge just a little bit.

My guesswork is not scientific, so always do your own research.

But the answer I do have is get back into the game of life, find the authentic you, and embrace who you really are. Be true to yourself.

RR&R

Here are the words that have changed your way of thinking. Review them daily, and feel encouraged in knowing that you are transforming into the person that God wants you to be.

Remember, there is power in our spoken words. Choose your words carefully, and enjoy your newfound strength.

REPAIR
FORGIVENESS
ASK IN PRAYER
HUMBLE THYSELF
BEND
HEAL
NO
BOUNDARIES
GRATEFULNESS
COMPASSION
TEARS TO FILL A RIVER
NO VICES!
DON'T CURSE OTHERS OR YOURSELF
BE STILL, BRIDLE YOUR TONGUE (THIS IS THE HARDEST ONE), LEARN TO LISTEN

RESTORE
RESPECT
APPEARANCE
GOALS
PASSION
RELATIONSHIPS
HOME
HOBBIES

RECLAIM
DREAMS
COMMITMENT
INTEGRITY
MORAL COURAGE
CHANGE

You are a blessing, and you have a sense of purpose; use it to do good and make a difference.

Finishing the Race

As you come to the end of this book, you have had the opportunity to really look at your situation and see that through all the pain, there is a new beginning awaiting you. I pray that you have gotten a clear vision of who you are and what you need to do to make the changes in your life a reality. Life lessons will always teach us who  we are, what we are made of, and how we handle the end result. It is all a test; the pain is real, and the brokenness inside can be healed, but we have to stand up and reclaim what is ours. You have taken the first step; just remember it does not happen in one day. It will take a journey of RR&R along with PP&P, but don't give up. You are more than a conqueror, and the best is yet to come. Learn from your mistakes, and move forward to your new beginning.

I hope that you have used this book as a journal and have written key words and thoughts of how you feel. Why this is so important is that you will look back in several months and read your words and see where you have grown. Look at your goals that you set for yourself and see how all has lined up for your good.

Even though with this breakup there was no makeup, you had to wake up, and it has created a life-changing journey for you. Embrace the pain and the lessons; reinvent yourself, and get living and enjoying your life again. You have done the work, and you have something special to bring to the table. Just don't forget who you are, and have boundaries. Don't just give yourself away. You are special, and don't let anyone take that away from you.

Remember you can't change time, but time can change you, one sunrise at a time.

God bless.
PHJ xoxo

Index